E

WORKBOOK
FOR
THE SIMPLE PATH
TO WEALTH

(A Guide to JL Collins' Book)

The Effective Guide to Creating and Following a Good Road Map to Financial Independence for a Rich, Free Life

A QUICK LOOK INTO JL COLLINS' LIFE

Mr. Collins provides straightforward, practical information and resources to help you understand investing with confidence in his book, "The Simple Path to Wealth: Your Road Map to Financial Independence and a Rich, Free Life."

JL Collins worked mostly in the publishing industry, but this is nearly irrelevant to his overall legacy. What really mattered (to him and to us today) was his relentless pursuit of F-you Money. He claims that personal independence ranks highest among the many things money can buy.

In 2011, he started his blog, jlcollinsnh.com, to document these and other lessons he wished to pass on to his daughter. To his amazement, it has expanded from those early days to become a global phenomenon. The Stock Series posts have made it popular.

He also thinks stocks, and more especially, broad-based index funds, are the best way to develop wealth. In addition, they constantly go up.

Although most investors lose money doing so. This seeming paradox is addressed by JL Collins in his book and blog, where he also instructs readers on how to use the market to their advantage in pursuit of financial freedom.

HOW TO USE THIS WORKBOOK

- Have a deep and sincere desire to do the things that is recommended here.

- Ponder upon and meditate on the food for thought, reflecting on how they relate to you, what you're advised to do and how to go about doing them.

- In the note section, write down important decisions you've made, relating to the things you've learnt.

- Don't discard this book when you're done with the 7 – Days Program. Instead, always have it in mind, never failing to return when you appear to be deviating.

- Make this a lifestyle. You'd find out that there was far more to gain in the main book through using this practical guide.

- Never assume that the lessons here are difficult and impossible to achieve, they're realistic and made easy for you.

- Follow the daily outline religiously, don't jump days or prioritize one activity over the other.

- Everything outlined here is important for you, don't neglect any.

- We recommend that you spread love and help with this workbook, give people whom you feel would need it. It could go a long way.

ALL THE BEST AS YOU
VENTURE INTO THIS…..

1st DAY

FOOD FOR THOUGHT

When you carelessly spend money
without knowing what and where
you're spending each month, there's

great probability that you'd not be able to preserve wealth.

TASK FOR THIS DAY

Start monitoring your expenses in order to improve your financial lifestyle. Improve your spending awareness for better money management.

KEEP THIS TO HEART...

Using a money management app like MoneyTrack to keep watch of your spending would save you from lack.

IMPORTANT REFLECTIONS (NOTES)

_____

_____

_____

_____

_____

_____

_____

_____

_____

_____

_____

_____

PIN THIS!

People with financial maturity don't ever spend without budgeting.

2nd DAY

FOOD FOR THOUGHT

Money does not ever last just by mere saving. In fact, if you're not earning more money, then you're getting poorer. Reflect on inflation and how it devalues your savings.

TASK FOR THIS DAY

Check up your available fund and find a suitable investment to start. Even if your ability to invest is limited, making small contributions to investment accounts will earn you profit.

KEEP THIS TO HEART...

People who invest more than they save have reduced chances of ever going broke again. Always ensure that you're able to make more money from the ones you have.

IMPORTANT REFLECTIONS (NOTES)

_____

_____

_____

_____
_____
_____
_____
_____
_____
_____

PIN THIS!

Never let your spending to out pass your earning.

3rd DAY

FOOD FOR THOUGHT

Creating a realistic monthly budget is a cool financial lifestyle that'd save you from poverty. Put everything into consideration, knowing that you're a human being with needs.

TASK FOR THIS DAY

Make a nice budget that'd cover for your moderate lifestyle, enjoyment, savings and investment.

KEEP THIS TO HEART...

Budget for everything, don't subject yourself to unnecessary pain and don't live too lavishly.

IMPORTANT REFLECTIONS (NOTES)

_____
_____

_____
_____
_____
_____
_____
_____
_____
_____

_____

<u>PIN THIS!</u>

Have a defined amount for your expenses.

FOOD FOR THOUGHT

Realize the fact that if you save money today, it'd save you tomorrow. Never neglect the powerful attribute of good saving culture.

TASK FOR THIS DAY

Form the habit of saving at least 20% of your monthly income. Save up continuously, even it'd take time to store up huge sums.

KEEP THIS TO HEART...

It's a very dangerous lifestyle to be without savings. Make sure that you have money at all times.

IMPORTANT REFLECTIONS (NOTES)

_____
_____

_____

_____

_____

_____

_____

_____

_____

_____

_____

PIN THIS!

How much have you saved so far?

5th DAY

FOOD FOR THOUGHT

It is never a wise decision to pay your bills late every month. Paying your bills early is a simple way to regulate your money wisely.

TASK FOR THIS DAY

Whenever a bill comes up, endeavor to pay it up before it gets late.

KEEP THIS TO HEART...

Paying your bills early gives you ample opportunity to plan your finances.

IMPORTANT REFLECTIONS (NOTES)

_____

_____

_____

_____

_____

_____

_____

_____

_____

_____

_____

PIN THIS!

Outstanding debt prevents proper financial planning.

FOOD FOR THOUGHT

Do you subscribe to some services you never use? It's usual and easy to forget about monthly subscriptions.

TASK FOR THIS DAY

Research and unsubscribe to recurring charges you never use.

KEEP THIS TO HEART...

Recurring charges that are not being used drain your money. They prevent valuable budgeting and render you broke.

IMPORTANT REFLECTIONS (NOTES)

_____

_____

_____

_____

_____

_____

_____

_____

_____

_____

_____

PIN THIS!

Always make sure that all recurring charges are being used.

7th DAY

FOOD FOR THOUGHT

In order to maintain wealth, you don't have to be extremely sentimental with people. You shouldn't help every single person because you yourself could get broke by doing that.

TASK FOR THIS DAY

Start saying no to demands that will not favor your finances and budget. Don't accept to help every single person.

KEEP THIS TO HEART...

One person cannot help every person.
You need to be selfish sometimes as
you build your life.

IMPORTANT REFLECTIONS (NOTES)

_____

_____

_____

_____

_____

_____

_____

_____

_____

_____

_____

_____

_____

_____

_____

PIN THIS!

Don't let yourself to be manipulated in this wicked world.

CONGRATULATIONS!

YOU MADE IT TO THE END OF THE 7 DAYS PROGRAM.

IMBIBE THE THINGS YOU'VE LEARNT AS A LIFESTYLE!

Made in the USA
Middletown, DE
09 August 2024